Songs from a Mountain

Amanda Nadelberg

Coffee House Press
Minneapolis
2016

Coffee House Press books are available to the trade through our primary distributor, Consortium Book Sales & Distribution, cbsd.com or (800) 283-3572. For personal orders, catalogs, or other information, write to info@coffeehousepress.org.

Coffee House Press is a nonprofit literary publishing house. Support from private foundations, corporate giving programs, government programs, and generous individuals helps make the publication of our books possible. We gratefully acknowledge their support in detail in the back of this book.

LIBRARY OF CONGRESS CATALOGING-IN-PUBLICATION DATA

Names: Nadelberg, Amanda, author.
Title: Songs from a mountain / Amanda Nadelberg.
Description: Minneapolis : Coffee House Press, 2016.
Identifiers: LCCN 2015033492 | ISBN 9781566894340 (softcover)
Classification: LCC PS3614.A28 S65 2016 | DDC 813/.6—dc23
LC record available at http://lccn.loc.gov/2015033492

PRINTED IN THE UNITED STATES OF AMERICA

23 22 21 20 19 18 17 16   1 2 3 4 5 6 7 8

I'm expressing my inner anguish through the majesty of song.
—Ron Burgundy

• • •

Contents

• • •

Songs from a Mountain

Emigrant Gap

Festooned and the sea,
as if the start of a leave
were none other than
a bone before the
shore: lilacs delivered.
(If I saw the sun I was
happy.) The bridge not
stuck so much as standing
well, where it does, what
is any of this but that, a
point for kings coming to
see what happened in the
sleeping years they were
I was gone. Fielded bottles
and still flowers, yes, the
store, yes, my discontent is
back. I say the singer has his
turn on the moon.

Oyster and Overture

In Denmark of all places it was snowing
on Cape Cod, replete with essays of the
month attempting normalcy. The new
mantra—see more legs—was I'm proud
of you, doing what in the empire regions
of a Dutch state, caring to handle things
that flutter. Persistence cues the weather
never long and troubled driveways,
emblematic grave-boat essay notwithstanding.
Wild rains the woods, don't get attached to the
evenings, stories and their cars, falling down a hill.

The concept is birds coming at the sea—in
other words, the western galaxy plays music
making Sunday (and all other days there are
for particular pleasures) seem like wind socks
finding nothing while feigning a good show.
Do you know what I mean, birds
without soul parts, clean sisters neither
here for count nor handling? Cue the house
resisting cheer, plain offing its doors in the
lily pond, spraining a dream memory. Cue
animals, dissipating fervor, falling on the valley
white, love, there's no sign of change. Consumed,
clipboards break away, they aren't seals but men, men
men men, waiting for the eddy as standing permits.

This debut happening is the snow above the house
convincing time to undress regardless of shame.
The people waiting in the water, going down in
the water, the starved power of salt running on the
beach, the chorus of men in the sea. There was
a man interested in summer, constructing a house
on the fallacy of what we slept on the floor. Some
light made afternoon say—among the colors of the
season in the sky that wouldn't stay—eventually
we become unmanageable. It was a low moon,
out an embarrassed room, the new season of the city
was mauve, it was black. Being uncertain as something
to do, went to the desert and did it.

Matson

The flowers were Asiatic Lilies and
I decided to call them Delphiniums

I don't drink the juice in California
it's not just the environment it's also
litigation, daylighting the chemicals
some of my best friends use mirrors

Caspian siren, you leave first, stash
letters in their boxes—my mother
says memoir funny, I imagine plants
and mishear the rapture—when you
forsake me, don't think I won't tell
my country; dear Mondrian, enter
these then go on. Call them vessels
in air. There was the Internet again

Spring my father says he felt intensity
or possible violence in my friend, I tell
him it's a barking cough. 8-10 women
describing cleavage, I won't just like it
because you ask me to, like day or a
nesting smatter of bridled ephemera
I hop up more knots, remember how
Spirit got its wheels stuck in the sand
my fifth-grade classroom as the visual
representation of current events. (The
desks wobbled.) Mornings I walk and
my friend talks me across desert-lined
jujubes until we can't recall having lost
the cosmos or how we got to be this
affluent in our feelings, I ask her: but
has he any positive experiences in love

So what patent reason is there to doubt
the color of a person's hair, there is sun
and timpani. Rubber wood bone silk
hemp or ivory I will cut my own in June
but in May endured the next yesterday
I've already now forgotten what all the
men I'll ever know smelled like. Maybe
devotion on the beach in the middle of
the week which is dumbed down with
planets imagining song. So I stopped
making port paintings when I heard the
neighbor's petite girlfriend coming
home, opera night, go back to writhing
with the sun, Kathryn, I have a question
what shape would you call the fall? Any
of us looking for answers in mid-light
learning to be a little mindful of the fever
of the mode. If I'm the rain we spend $
on a Tuesday to never spend money on
other things. (I lost my way.) Hey, I'm
the clouds without thinking without time
or intention. Sometimes they just want
to pull you into it, and it isn't money, not
when we're talking in leads. He couldn't
wait to tell the women what he'd done for
days. I felt so alone playing house with a
stranger, my house speaks better at night—I
was listening to the house with a stranger, I'll
be here when you come. The leaves sound
Haydn, then darkness. I liked his cadence that
it demonstrates kindness or that we might have
misplaced our surfaces. I imagine my life

Frank delivery at the door (blanket / coat)
the phone is getting wet, my friend writes
he's not going anywhere, if you need me

I'll be analog; my mother and sister in a
Calvert's in Massachusetts, 1986, I was
under a rack then descending some stairs
to a basement room of jeans. Is anything
residential? I showboat the apartment you
carried upstairs in a dream to me but of
you I like best the part not saying a thing
sitting here next time beside me looking in
a direction of light. Your shoes off, the hour
having disturbed duration; you couldn't press
ahead however often you try. So a man I ride
the bus home with when I don't wish to go
spells the alternate circles of streets and I'm
Zelda again; in Nintendo we call this next
level but in Berkeley they mark hills. Or some
films are about children, they're not dead yet
and they're going somewhere. Westward, how
I don't value the conception of anything, sun
happening regardless of clouds. (I'll wait to get
berries with my sister.) The room gets quiet
in time for a stanza in which you touch me
plant my hair, yes, I catalog my days. (Recall
when I couldn't walk and slept in a strange
bed?) The house is perfect for the fact of its
one room, its windowpane wall, actual leaves
outside singing, the kitchen running east
into other people's yards under stars (as if
I'd baked lavender, besides, commissioned
light conveys an ease of appetite). In the
a.m. Valentina improves with more room
between her buttons than before, getting
ready in time while reducing distractions
from light, noise and pets. We don't need
to be friends any longer I tell the sycamore
before they're cut down. The wick for the
hinterland, wonder, anyone and their parents

manipulating death, I saw movies before I
was transposed to the city, I was not a real
cinematographer but I cared, each minute
thinking who is it, who is it. Some green
order of supplemented fear I like the sound
of the cyclists mining the pavement while
professionalizing stones. The light won't
go down when Canada is singing to me or
you now. To not know your brother or to
believe in other tenets to have a tub to run
home (I repeatedly tell myself I don't need
to know) to hang flowers to walk him to the
gold theater to bury a friend in the garden to
count to eleven to name the days of the week
otherwise to leave the dishes there to harp
on your friends to grace a table to smell new
tires on my sister's car to romance the small
apartment to be retrospect to believe in your
maybe to have a fit when you come or make
me to be hardly one to be handy in love or to
love a movie enough to have seen it too many
times to write a letter to write an actual letter
and to put a letter in the eventual mail or to
lean over to resolve oneself to know the ether
to see a spit of night left through the trees

The efficiency of matches began this inquiry
when the man walked cowardly. It was then
that I wondered what a person is to do with
heavy light, electric thrummed star, I cannot
be blamed for our daughters on the sea
a song for the blue or beige lights adorning
the mind as votel potpourri. The object
is to stop at some point and the shape
pulls the breaks ahead. I had friends in
other pews they weren't on my train

and I missed them, I was busy driving
lavender for days, I don't buy flowers
or think to, I bought myself a pink vase
and cake for Jane. Immune to hollyhock
or ivy searing finer days I could look
at the sky and see leaves then remember
the limitations of my friends; I have no
need for trivial conversation and the
intensity exhausting a world, can you
bear it, can you bear children he asked
me on the mouth as we crossed the street
I played the part of the sweater. Of wonder:
what to do with radial photographs at night
when it's plum season and the animals on
the porch are aping us; spitting cherry pits
down I wash my tracks off the pavement by
2960 Linden Street, heaven, he taught me
to pronounce the names of rosemary and
jasmine, I think aloud retroactively what
ails you, doorway, because your cocky
posture alone imagines a mute sky and
if aloneness creates its own desire then
send me back in mapped envelopes. (I
will pull down those lemons myself.) The
shop is open Sunday, and sure the place
is ugly but I could love there. 36, let's
say then? But how would I know if
I forget to forge normalcy, he smelled like
bread and declined to ride a bike. When
the fridge quiets down I'll tell you about
my cousin and what we talk about some
of the time, the friend of my friend is
not a friend necessarily and when the
fridge turns back on I'll be annoyed, a
white belt calling you from a machine into
the world. I don't care toward time, which

is only a barbarian breach of honor and
decency before Mazzini & the poppy seeds
or a woman named Merlin calls and I answer
and before I knew to write a poem called
"After Okn for Ben Estes" and before this
moment of the fridge again. Then there
is San Francisco burdening, plumb faces
dirty with sun. (He was a form developed
by star storms.) Hell, I was ready to give up
all the music and pictures the night the
rain sounded like a burglar. In the world
interrupting I wonder what we're doing, that
while my own mother was 59 I worked in
an ice cream store, or how I love her now
more evenly, my father too, keenly read
how they confound the line of propensity or
narrative, how they still sound at my door. My
sister and I wanted mansions, vain and foolish
the wrath. (Is that Zeus?) If I'm allowed to think
in the god-purse and if I'm met in the sun where
my form is often shaking on cue beside a forest
of soaped-over windows and if you are, with
me, what I believe you ordinary to be in the
prerecorded sounch of our consequential days
stalking the caveats of alphabets, I delete our
boat tracks because what offers them is not for
sinking hills into foragers or tendered points
for each of the times that any two of us said
hey. It's for horses if you take off your
films in the future, historically, when I will
remember what mornings it first seemed
approaching an object, dumb heat from the
machine rustling the body. The Internet says
next week is approaching the 80s but I'd
prefer to get back to the TV nightly news
in fact, I'd pay heaven to see what sort of adult

I'd be now then. (Two Dutch uncles walk into
a bar. Scene.) Relevance marks the lack of
sound in the mechanical snow, it's become so
hollow in this yearlong symphony and now I ask
him to exhibit more uncertainty, I've denounced
myself I tell myself that I don't need to know I
could watch you do nothing and press me out
I am here, can you hear me Polo. (I'm taking
all the snow.) In 1991 the governor said what we
count (and need) is our business and a nameless
storm dressed my family in candles and rain and
my mother spilled (red) wine on someone else's
(white) couch while *Arachnophobia* got lodged
in the underworld of the VCR. Power that backed
onto days in which my brother (that brother) had
his hair and time. I was nine and spoke mostly in
affirmations to my elders. I trust him to dial down
when able, to cut the sea into practical parcels
of fabric to lower the lens of daylight to speak
into his own milled sousaphone unhinged, lit ends
but what we share isn't contraband it's stupidity
and surreptitiously at that, until a table is witness
to a plaid response to a sunken thought I'd been
having with myself. (These containers stack up on
my way to the city.) The neighborhood eats in the
street to indicate an American holiday. I have
my wall of sound and fire sticks pretending, my
orange couch and paintings, the fridge turns off
again. Helen in the corner, dead all these years
and Angela and Mariah and Ben. I'm a bell no
more, would you munder the beer would you
bandit my comb, would you have onto me
for days of devotion and hem I'm not confusing
the bower for making the street endlessly
hold a ladder beneath heaven. Hills mine
I talk to any day again, embarrassed to speak

unless it's from a mountain or behind the lilac
screens and I don't remember what song used
to pull me through a room like this or any other
willfully misunderstood. Let me go again into the
epileptic air that will render a body capable or
less dumb to the sun signaling its framed song; I
would erase the fog from your mouth if you come
closer to the cocanned mountain I'm calling from
if you translate your measures into fairer kindling
that would be days if you let them light onto you

You've made me nervous until you don't, and it's my
light. Three white horses, maybe in another country
children, at least time. That it could be furtive talk
regardless it let me, like mechanical shipping animals
belong to industry, say aquifer or Heidegger and
watch him pose with his family. (I look like this each
day.) White is forever a dumb color on women, blood
Floridian, I spent ten daughters on his misdirected
tenderness and the clarity might have feigned the desk
toward silence you can't address a self from, you
wild concierge. When putting buttons on my neck, he
need have care for it's my only and part of loneliness has
to do with certain faces of money especially when I ask
what to bring to the spare curfew. (Sinking on cue, Cathy
Pacific begins her memoir.) Now to believe he was a
catalyst, if adventure means leaving the apartment
then send me the bill from Antarctica, my favorite house
is on Hammond Street and at all times looked like it
will have withstood one hundred fires. When the cost
washes enough I tell mother to buy. The wind is
dark and sounds hectic, I don't care to be so infected
so as to lose friends who say I can't see until I can say
all things again. I close the window on buses and the
clothes at the mall. You follow each other because the
king me'd beauty is such that my eyes hurt, Pacific

Coast Container scene lunging every afternoon. Late
in the month the netted books talk into the way day
here always begins like a weak song, one worth bidding
to handle. (It was my shining moment in which I shined
and you were being an asshole.) The questionnaire
asks whose face do you see when choking, I will sit
this one out I tell the made platoon, which is accurately
an aviary of sensory diagrams pulling our features
along. 34 years more into the hollow graph ratifying
the imaginary buildings our people abandon their lives
into. To the sound of all canopies waving, meet me at
the rectory I'll be the mute dressed in blue. This example
of my vacant handle has everything to do with confidence
(personal, *see also* a lack of) and the use of a phone. I
had not even thought of Hawaii, some idea in the sea—it
let me go—but you could be in Marin, the light staking
its way. My stars so to speak. One magic peddle reigned
in the factory when I refused to look down, the little
prince knitting breakdowns. (Then speak whence he did
ushering toward.) By Matson the train's speed comes
to a new sound. In 1946 my mother was born to
a woman who gave me my legs. Footsteps colliding
the pavement to charge the music again, imitation clocks
tour time in which I lie down whether or not the
singer finds the place she tries for when the bar talk
consumes a summer of myself. (In the midst I call
Jessica who is home.) That it took my fav'rite singer ten
plus seven years to log under a condition of weather
before shredding for his own name makes the brilliant
dream in which he tells me I'm wonderful all the more
a signature for both parties involved. The keg is still
standing in the basement where you left it six years ago
under a garden's collapsible song. I'm pretty sure
I saw his brother on a Sunday train. Speak, arrow, my
heirloom on a post, the lamp near repair, the fridge
saying again when three letters stood for lessons and

not a blackened compromise, poor adherence or
rough banks against anyone's grave mouth. Oh
Arden, I took you for a lakefront

My father remembering his first memory as scared
in a rubber tube (VT) small and unable to return
to the shore, I know the photo and the fact of having
myself to understand he survived. In the symphony
now there are 5 hoverings in a simple web and there's
some magi joshing with the oft eternity of green
leaves. If things are shifting it's because summer
suspends me until I push the curtain back to see
what's really been said, it's too easy to undo our
documented mistakes but the fable wrecks your
chances for me to care, I can't anymore I'm a
spent door opening you. The dentist's daughter
catalogs (13 is missing) woke up of two minds
social and appalled, stuffing the weekend light
into my bosom which is hereby a euphemism
for docks, or wonder, the table listening yet holds
questions of your mossing intentions which, haunted
nowadays, have proved off-putting to the glory that
was time when I knew you were decided from
the stars (20 is missing) and I know where I am
in the blue of the map but can't promise you
contrast if you don't note the shore every few
ounces so I might light my head under that
fire kicking. Pacifica gold smolts the day because
it sounds good, murderous plums in their pre-fall
which means difficulty is as much as it is to feel
something across multiple bodies, each weekend
becoming the next in terms of essay. (This isn't
going well.) Greek memories, some cat plundering
fences, pay the woman in her pink dress, to know
the cunning flowers on Wednesday, bubbled-in
windows of ash, no, this end of the earth

If I motion scissors to muse will it suffice? Zeus
let me afford the small house here, its zoned flowers
pickling space, however interrupting his sensation
appears. Painting remains in the market of my walls
as enough politics I'll admit in the cacophony of
the mild hamlet. His confusion belies him, to have
ability is to have regular blood in the street when
there are people in love who eventually become
grown animals in the park. (In English I can say
I don't want to be with someone only to argue
nor do I want it to be about you.) Elegance dying
its hair, it will rain tonight if you're careful
which I am more than I should be, my doctor
sending handwritten notes. Green copping
waves to the floor and the wind walking trains
I've learned in precise increments

The theory is because it's a painting is why it hangs
together, the vestments' understudy barging her head
into a tree. (You listened until you didn't and I left
the room.) Consider the California Soda Co. on the
way or a peanut coming to the city; in this frame
be the peanut. The plain act of consisting that makes
decisions in a bottle. And how he was losing
his keen sense of conception

So if summer was a sundered form high-tiding
each day, was its accomplice in the dream part
a city set up by my units measuring false and epic
memories? White lawn, porch scenes, rotunda

The doors wouldn't open, and at MacArthur the
conductor restarted the train, pushing a button.

Of Oceans

In this that there will be no sounding some water
part of the world, the morning, without mistake
for sleep how else could they have claimed, bright
sweater, that you're unfortunate, standing by a tower
daring the mad sea away.

When they put erotic under stone, a bed of hair became
the ocean; when the ocean transformed to another
as likely, I told you, go ahead and sing yourself.

And why, when I shut my eyes I see houses in fields
I can't say; but know they are beautiful, lit from
within, song lamps, the heaven in the rooms on fire.

                              While
tightly the car turns down the road, headlight love,
the sentence holds itself to face, claims solidarity
with energy, lie downs and Romans everywhere;
no dreams of dining halls: assumptions have
a little death each time we let them out, windows shine
at home, lakes stealing into pockets that aren't yours,
as if chairs had desires of monks losing time.

Wharf toward the city lights at night the hills on
fire, bridge unwilling, announcing the future
of oceans, an island in a river, a headboard
a husband, a second-story window, I think you're
thinking of me as I do you, swimming in the evening
with a sandwich on the dock, footwear like the
charm of collapsing houses, I'll sit with you but
I want your chair.

The breath
of the room on trees outside the window,
chairs packed up like the voice of influence,
summer will horrend itself on us; I stop myself,
no decent way to sit in a forest by the tender
lines to think about all we've done. There are
roads, they're beautiful, and I will see you.

As far as it can throw, not
fair, death coming, it does, the chair talks back, I
hush the room; breakfast potentially anyone's dalliance,
I don't know why I check the sky, it's still there, working
by impossible diary light, and you're fine, here
in any season you come up with.

Alcove for waking up to pixel nights, or reasons a
person listens, a car fitting hands, alcove of the body
as a green room, a forest of indelible fishing lines of
thought, like a bundle of rooms undone, not ready,
I will furnish you, let you over. Staircases imagining seas
at night, the streets quiet invisible us; when you climb
the stairs and my hand on the door, and I open the door,
and greetings expected and all of you in your button-down
shirts, all of you singing, all of you nightly, all of you
standing next to the fridge, cornering a piece of the night.

Linear Motor

I am here for my sister with a voice
like a boat if it wasn't the first time
someone had given me a present
they wanted. Tuesdays are hard for
me, he wasn't calling me babe, in
August and after Dorsky, sitcoms as
someone's brother. I left my house to
ride the pedestrian wave, ever since
procedure there is in me a sea. Of
orchids and peasants, moss became
an echo laced by the front door
sounding furious to its own dim
hands. *Incremona!* there is no color
but things, I work with my feelings or
his red bicycle. (Line.) It took weeks
to clear up the mess, what I have is my
mouth I think to the women passing.
I still need buttons from the store.
History moves in circumstantial years
as artless practice for later entrance
ports. This is about that. Explanatory
holy work in the depths.

Siren

In which a lack of curiosity about yourself makes you wonder
    what I look like in pictures at night
The neighbor without regard for the mote that anticipates disruption
It's my sink after all
To try again, take off your socks
In which we can't go to some awful museum
In which I refuse to be friends with false rules
Distance as the machine of mockery the first three
    collections need some slowing down
In which Dickens permeates songs writ by women in tattoos
In which you have come to be a deeper idiot maneuvering light

In which I am the man I want you to be coming
The light now, like Petra
I never saw how the inside of the elevator on California flickers
Accumulation and piecemeal of callous ecstasies on the wall I was a child
In which my friends have fallen into salty days
In which there are false tales
In which I go to a bar on the corner and I take off my dress and someone plays
    "Rich Girl" by a band called Hall & Oates
Ribbons in the northern parts of Caroline and the sky or Colorado in July
The pouring fan
The collateral of rational loans or laughter
Let me talk about pink sky before it gets in Saturn's way

In which the state park lets in dogs, the natural world, betting
In which one person has legs and the other doesn't
A night colliding when you look for a number and color to indicate life
In which I swim out and call your name from under the water
The night refrigerated what goods we had I was twenty-one, loved him,
    in a window built to warm a room near Canada

In which I dream and there are dreams of Ashbery wearing brown
Her feet on the stairs not unlike the tenuous state we inhabit
In which the wild will go further on sale
If someone laced an object to my door it smelled like actual love
In which I put my friend's child to bed
The vacuum sounding the potential of the building

In which I walk by the ferries to smell the tourists and bread
In which the coffee table is a microwave and the sun is gone to fright
Electric parchment lights the days my parents are alive
Painters consumed by little knobs
In which the book was a natural world or I've worn the wind
In which tortoiseshell is a color and if it were
Consider the rain
In which my friend had traveled to the end of North America, a post office
    in the middle of a sea
A glass of water

In which a person identifies sayings and landscapes
I want to have traveled by car
In which the light is right and you're beside the instruments
It's a long way to the season we sleep in
I was waiting for rain
Roz smelled like a closet by the sea
I asked them to meet me at the rectory, they flew me to Italy, I was sixteen
I wonder to the screen
I wonder why he is up so late
I close the window when I don't like what it says
I prefer vulnerabilities
I don't know why they were there

Five-Day Present for Aunt Ollie

Having traveled together I was late, a
satchel full of purpose, stolen attempts
disrupting rooms and waking thought
with miscellaneous trips outside; in real life
I had no passport and you had no phone.
We relied on the little one to bring us
home, the beard drove his car
through an elevator and up, I was

late, and they would not wait for me.
There are people inside their blue houses.
April, a light on for most flowers.
March: I wasn't ready. The lamp like
a well, particle blushing rooms and
an important blue something-else in your
mind, maybe plaid, maybe a blanket making
the lots faced daily any easier to bear

I was there, I was plain hearted with a home
beneath the states that I put on, the sky
setting itself on fire. All these books,
they're too much! I'll not read them, no!
Let's send them back to the woman
who wrote them. I was eating breakfast
with my father when the news came
on, the walls were green, we were

having eggs. So many times we're
thrust upon ourselves and so what?
Well I was sleeping, then woke to the
cluttered sound of an old pine hitting the
garage, it was at once spectacular and
bad, as if ways of seeing were named

after a woman without sounding, or if
windows could buy themselves

outright, before centuries—I'd gladly
pay for the whole world to see
what could be done for elegance on
walls of different colors. Novel forms
are over but doubling back on the day
I found patterns. You were of the pattern
on the wind, it fell into our rooms
without asking.

Aphrodite Goes Baroque

If I broke it
the string light
in opposition
to the form of
seeing you like
you are and at
that a collection
of letters ordered
by the sun

The Third Principle

In lieu of flowers
for the market,
I keep my teeth
I sew my song
I wring the day.
Having never owned
such an arrangement
I don't know how it ends
this long song of articles, the soul
experiments in miraculous play.

Entry of the sleep flame brings
the score beneath today; king me
a heated machine, a bit of certainty
from the war. Maybe no music
says day to the lavender doom.
Here where I was prepared
for method, counting reeds for
the want of it because time is likely
always at night.

Able Seaman

or if a name were a spell
in binding letters called
fields and you caught
onto me with a name like
that the slight gray nymph
riding skies at night, tossed
by the fifth day of the week
which is to say on a Thursday
I came to you in a dream
capshaw, a pocket note of
posies pulling anyone's sweater
in the right direction, off into
the nettles when what happens
if I get there first, a face
returning leisure from places
of nevertheless, an industry

Gornisht Means Nothing

                        I don't know
the rule I'm supposed to follow but frankly
nor do I care. The space turned itself out
when it declared I AM NOT SPAIN. Fire, or
some electric sign, a brothering, like a row
of grown-up sisters, to the sounding thirst
I bade farewell, unnecessary acrobat unloved.

Of the mouth we chose ribbons: wallops painting
Tiburon, rock crystals forming in the mind of
an antler. Just as birds do enter gladly, a private
city will sing anywhere that heights turn cold
in the morning—we argue enough or
not at all. Blame the children, their questions

all that's left to fill the light, an old door
doubles like a doorbell sounding Italian,
sub-country phrases subpoenaed to sleep;
O illiterate meadow: if I had stars, had
charged them tonight or if light was a fixture
of tractors, streets might find their sound

resistance debatable: look how women
run into the world, the gold bangs of a
window wanting to be brought inside.
The doorbell feigns broken, too many lights
on at home there is nobody I'd rather eat
lunch with but that's not true anymore.

Some women put things into a basket
but this fumble on the bench, it's not
for me. When I was yours my arms
were longer and grammar was all we

needed. Now that I'm the theater I'm
tired, I pretend that I'm not listening,
pretend that I am Spain, and like mothers
let night-lights let rivers make the sounds
those interpreters might help us remember.

Mont America

i.

Give me an address
married in the snow.
Bell-tram incantations
on the riverboat mind,
a song for boatpeople,
a double sonnet for love,
holding aprons you will not look bad.
People know Sunday. Did I say I hear a symphony.
Honey to blouses won't catch a lion bird
in den grown legs. Like a man I'm thinking
like two movies at the same time, both classics
in the American sense of the word. American
I am an animal, saw the sea and five seals surfacing
because it was today, cloud dementum, daylight
caulking from no place audible, and the garages
I've parked in fields, errand dream: I have a windy
sister, a colliding mastery, this is my first in a series on
longing. I will be here 'til next Tuesday / will answer
questions during the break.

It was nothing if we were not ourselves
when life was a study of mantels behind
ears. A tender part of any story is a man in his
backyard in the world after the fires. Like a meadow
I am a little like a flower with a bothered throat, singing
impressions of tomorrow today under the influence of nothing and
Baudry, a trunk under new castles, catastrophe in the arbor,
van's persimmon. Turn your face from the country,
good posture in the mountain. Audrey a liar singing
the terror of love between two people is a film I've seen before.

A day unto itself a clean matter, allotment of ether.
See my brothers making noise in their houses.

Taking things out of context   to form a party   the dog dishwasher
who makes a Gypsy's day   brighter than the sun   avenge me death
death, an opera   who makes it   there are two sides to any story
pity misplaced I will save you or die   yours is a bag of opera

Unmistaken star bring us back a bevy of things from the shore.
Poland for instance. Our collarbone, your California rights,
two fattish men and a question.

See the blur chart: in a pod of seals I rolled the séance down the hill,
said wind, open, run along to the store. Adequate sundries for
albatross & air, parsnip: say I am the door, say not my body to the not future.

ii.

Whether the earth
Or the machines
I was the earth was
My wordless narrative
The infinite song
As much about
American buildings
As anything. Lodestars?
I hate the little stickers
That they put on all the
Fruit, let me say it another
Way, ruin the corporeal
Undoing of certainty.
Did anyone ever want
To be an island with him?
I'm looking for my artificial tears.
Arrivals from the country

There is more rock below
Heroes are hard to find.

iii.

What was important
when I landed in the field
someone comes to the door
from Texas. No, let me
come to you, he left a print on me.
It's not that TV is going away,
it's that we think of it differently

The salt roof, September
nurse, she said ready
and I did the baby out.
Unlikely we gave it linens

Fancy he clovered beds
capsizing knapsack days, I do,
how I hope you are pulled over
between the sitcom and the moon.
If I see a smaller cart I will take it

Romantic concerns
things to do with breasts:
      open a marble factory in the woods
      take a friend out for dinner
      introduce yourself to a neighbor
      buy milk, asparagus, change the oil
      consider the lepers again

A woman with Cheetos on a busy street wipes her hands on her office dress party,
whichever month you're reading this Christmas is coming

iv.

My king answers bull sand
potato hands he drives to the water
a sadder display of narrator washing
gold stars eyeing the ether at night.

It was the desert that did it for me, a sea of tumbled
dishes parading in the sun. Now that I'm not sure
is it all right if I stand here and listen to nobody?
Goodnight nobody, a bridge joking with rain.
Wish that you were less of anyone's conflagration
and more of a sweet treat falling from some
corner of Texas. You never really had a beard.

Ordinary with money and whatever
we buy with it. We used to buy rackets.
Phones are back TV is dead so what
if I want to be in bed. He was like
instruments. If I stood straight I could
see him looking toward where
I was or wasn't depending.

Everything comes from the finishing moon
considering white, running the homesteads back
that is the country at night. In the middle of doorknob families
I am I am I am I am and I don't even know what comfort is.
If I fall down in the middle of the woods it will not be with a candelabra.

Tgus Gas Veeb

Truth be told the animals spent morning
all the ways one could with an earth,
if not of blurred affection then happy
circumstance; there's known reverse
fog on the hills when my friend comes
back to town, I put another wasabi snack
up to the monument, it's expensive and
I have no money. (The city pretending on
me.) Columbo nights recall that the bartender
walks home in the middle of the country and
the middle of the street some birds. This might
be what is happening in the linchpin of my
memory for last night the car couldn't get up
the wet hill, the hill was really a wave. What
else negates a lucid story if I'm in love with
a stranger's lisp. Some cars pass twice;
a song's uncertainty. I wish you weren't so
capitalized in the fog, not after all this salt.

Husband, Comfort, Aficionado

Anticipation don't emote me from
the mountain, long boiled millennia
calling from the middle of a tender sea
like goldenrod. Austerity waiting in the
sun, in seasons for lights to flick on, God,
I've arranged what I want a woman to be
continuously sighing don't do drugs on
me. (I don't recall whose hair I braided
but I did a fine job.) Jean-Paul Belmondo
playing a Ben from second grade with
radioactive likeness. I decided to let
the train get my body to the city that I
eschew but hours a day, how may I direct
your call? Willfully I'm certain now
there is everything and a corresponding
sea. Purple flowers tall as tendency, they
have tickets for the theater. The bed
a painting what do you want from me.

Love Ad Infinum

I will tell you a story of vanity
and illustrate a consequence from
two thousand years ago, when
we watched movies in the dark.
I said in morning there is no light.
When we argue it will be about
money or how to distinguish liturgy
from front lawns. To think it's hot
in the summer in Toronto was the
subsequent focus of a controversial wind
condescending to rapt seedlings, just
as any sewn place fields abstract green.
Soaking lucid perpetuity in the farmer's
animals' minds, a clean song, full grass,
I was attracted to those stars.

Money / Talks

O that common verb.
Dress me in spatulas
put the moon around
my neck. Parting air the
poet waves a hand, too
much lace and I wonder
if the trolley's real, a giant
upside-down flying spoon.
God and hair I knew you
in the Mechanical Age. Now
I am someone who gets off
and on trains with dads and
bags every day. Look, it's 4:43
in the afternoon people go
home. My mother wore
Obsession in the eighties.
I smell fire which has no
hands, did you hear me? I
have no horses now. Someone
did not make your sweater,
someone didn't make it
who loves you.

Novel Iron Works

Excused to undergo a body, having
starved the correspondence can't
remember what did I say. According
to the bracelet I fell asleep and in the
morning considered the cost of a new
foot, electric tumbleweed and gold
marionettes, a woman standing in a
field with bags. (Scene.) My neck was
a muscle in the California year to
render sleep not done was the man
disinterested in taro and the traffic
of his feelings? If a body began again
her voice cuts through glass. Not
suicide exactly but a form of willing
the lights to turn off. Feather mousse
bottle, white lavender, nothing could
be clearer and everything was.

The Illustrated History of the Universe (1955)

A woman who says I can't die
sooner than you will be noisy. Thing is
I have always been like this: emergent
denominations or how any of us negotiate
particles of love with flowers budding
from our necks, malfeasance on a day or
the falling part that has a lemon. Blindly
bumping into the self, Solomon was late
again for war. Correspondence, the signs on
faces my dreams keep coming to me, 3-D
glasses for the one sun, the sharp expression
of something falling from its body. Meet me
at home because the city makes me tired; the
sun comes and billows like sections. (Oh, here
it was.) In some age of pedantic use, strange
eggs walking, renaming paintings at museums
while studying color for idiosyncrasy when
I showered in the pew; I won't write about
women in heels I tell Chris and Dobby.

I Steal Care 4 U

Down from clouds directing
traffic misunderstood if needed.
So talk. You are tender or a movie
I am watching, can go whenever
you want between the unfinished
sentences colliding: cloud falsifying the
bear's soliloquy, ultimate performance,
I shush the fridge, wonder but if only
the dirt came less quickly into rooms,
the business of touching somebody: it
isn't that we need more information
it's that we need to step into the world
without our hands; if I seem stern
it's because I found myself looking
at the moon and seeing day laid out
in marshes, as if night were the entire
capacity for love. I'm not only night
I am also all the other things I've said.

Some city lights will draw bored movements
of people while grapefruit in the shower
is a phantom of the sea. I want to eat
alone. No más, I say to the Post-its confusing
the room. Old floor finds fault by the
door, cries delivery groom. The wave fields
wandering back and forth to Portugal

I miss my friends, they're heads of state,

of glory, kings of the arctic! A living thing

that may suffice like timing, or how the act

of putting your shoes on is a set of expectations.

Unremarkably we'll come to futures

in which plates and saucers lie in the sun,

the meadow lit with cakes. Related snow:

if I woke up thinking of a song in which

you touch me and go to bed again

then who killed the cook in the

drawing room? Where is Minerva?

It was the worst best times. Heat coming up

from the middle of the floor like podiums.

Hanuary denying our false progress: it said

hold onto me, bringing laundry to its knees

at the edge of a great Asian city. Metallic greens.

Expectation lay at the bottom of the tub,

I smelled bubble la mer. Please be sleeping

I thought as I thought there are four plays

in the world and in this I am the phone.

Against minnow and whale the sun

dressed like a shiny coin while my friend

danced softly, we are the trees, you

are naked, dying, I want to preserve

the man, willing the light, pushing the

buttons to turn on. I was and then I wasn't

a reasonable person, if regrettable, the face

of the building fell into the street, dealing
perspective in repeated but variable waves.

If it isn't day in the wall of sound,
Tuesday will sing. (Some songs never mind.)
Stolen hounds, our feet talking, winter
having been a hole in the ground or a staircase
caesura without its boat, I wait (here) for
a man to come in through the window
like a fax, slightly efficient. Her majesty's
best miracle a public garden (1963) the sign
proud in sunlight but cold and murmuring
just enough for a bridge. Like ventilation
things get better while they get worse, I left
my hair in the museum, and if I told you
I limped for a long time, that I didn't like
sunglasses but I liked my sunglasses.
At the museum which makes me feel
that I'm in trouble, a bill jar for what
I've dug into this week. I was a stranger
with money for a bridge. Again.

It is only a day like others asking that
any of us wake up, eat something
use the sun, go to bed. What else to do
with information but give it kindly; it
inspires. If a man leaves me and there is
no man is it a story? Or if I rake you over

a mountain, singing, O, look at the moon,

the romance of someone pronouncing

a whole name beyond introductions

would that be preferred? The painting is a

collection of lines forming the inside of

a painted cardboard box and if I could

wear it, Susan, I would. Jan's hair in the

snow, Jane's hair looks good in snow.

Who am I writing if not you, who am I

writing. During the melee Ben gets sand

from a barrel outside. Opal stands on lightning.

While my condition remains, I don't call.

Like he said, maybe we found another word

for bluebird. If you want to know how many

stars there are please leave me alone. Bring me

an envelope, Italians don't like puddles either.

I wish I'd been born in the mouth of a film, simple

flowers being best, money is stupid, I get up late,

like Petronius and a woman in white waves

a hand preciously. Sí a waltz runs through

your head, ride a tyger and you can't get off,

always these sycophants. Haydn plays over the

station beach, there are elevators in the air

and books on every shelf, and I ask you, what

tense is this, cinnamon? My room is the

same in every city, I am the same, have

brown hair, the coffeemaker, and drive a car.

The question rings at the door incessantly.
In my mind which sees the future I know
my friends will be in town.

Of all the small ends of the world I am
myself in this picture of the stairs, a box
apart from friends, getting limes in the dark
the sun a few minutes away, rushing the
condition from me. Ivan and a godwalk, people
don't play tennis in the rain, I can't move while
Misery is under the car. Cautious erstwhile the
daybooks green and blue, or meanwhile, painting.
Some menagerie of letters I've had with all of you.

Dear Woolsey Amis,

　　　When the rain stops be the treaty for night
and will the world into changing its news (grandmother,
porpoise, shell). Perhaps when the rain stops I will go.
Mother says because my mouth is small and
my teeth don't have a lot of room, my mother says
the world but she has foolish ideas. Perhaps
I allow myself to say things more than once,
I don't want to be surprised; in the summer, Balthazar.

Symphony of Leaves

Someone had bread pudding;
the end. Set rules of
no dancing, modal waves
of notes listing to the east.
Gutter then the stars. The
one to the left, let that be
mine, between the jukebox
and the door I loved you then
there will be more seasons
at the Gap, come back later.

Behind my stereo army acute
I stage a wondering; that's
what the coasts become,
someone is calling, blue light
blue asking for a green
light on a screen. Oh, you've
been to Sweden? Yellow hair
window she looks like shit
in a dress. Hey, your heart is a
fucking liar bleeding in the snow.

A personal hole, in a hole in the ground
if that's a place to live then I'm dead
                              exceeding light

If the earth opens on other shores
if I believe that music decides
the selection or if a man is
chasing a woman or if she is plain
faster than the man. Other
people's benders are good for
the economy just as defensive
sound strategies involve a lot

of NPR. They made me believe
that god was listening. How

young when a temple was the
tarmac; my mother has bones.
If you do a thing well enough
it doesn't matter whatever you
look like, this is America
and especially if you're a man
in your country (I'll run outside
you are love without thinking).
Gray-fashioned car, sky feigning
rooms, waiting. I use spoons.

Décor as an industrious time
idle afternoons into any others
we can't pick or choose
time like planted light
                beside itself with color

To the desert again to the
forest when I collapse I see.
Owned some amount of death
they looked like accordion
hearts, countered hands, those
are swans he says to the fixture.
You can't see what happens between
the skies; pocket full of doldrums
or maybe I just came back from
the country, Lilliputian lite.

O say more they're beautiful
(a road to the sea to feel, sing)
the refrigerator's small war.
A day named for daughters
or a man running tenuously, half
marm half monster a wild thing

in the woods. We've been chalking
fixes between one house and others,
portioned middling hellos, reason to
nod at disaster riding his bike at night.

Nive birds

As it transcribed, months planted
the faculties of simple affection
in a field of dresses and principled
men unencumbered on the
beach. This area was desert
twenty liens ago, the moon
like canopy discussed
selfishly. Do you believe
that still life could catch itself
at odds with the law? I suggest

we end all scenes of winter lots
parked yelling, that you keep your
hands dithering, count to twelve,
close your mouth or swallow up
the traditions of all things, mistakes
in the tally the ocean, for example
with no intention but something
of a seam ripping into the sky.
Witnesses will see twice the
effect it has on day. The canopy.

Nive birds singing

Against sleep / talking spells
a man, I don't know hell. Filling
the heavenly sprite, we throw
continuums under sound trains.
In honor of day people garner

accounts of time: moon stains
on the eddies, unnamed colors
in perceptible blight. Family
is a concept without regard .
for story, when I ask, say

apples invented the sun and that
bronze is your uncle. Minorly
maybe more is what we're missing.
I found tunnels and only in Boston,
and only on the way to an airport.
Or what I wonder, what you can get
for $500,000, what Oliver Stone
looks like on a summer night. A town
seizing last orders in the manic brigade
counting ourselves to be thimbles.

A bridge goes into me, publicly, the
front room of an old house, seventeenth-
century shade, the only way I know to save
                          money is to stay in

If all broke free O mordant earth,
if the rings of Saturday were on our lips
or there are sleeping people no place
in the sanctuary, the dew knotted
horses agreeing to meet at seven
by the sea. I repeat. Beer is
not a woman though clearly part
of an American conscience,
we think about the moon and
then none of us go outside.

Lo, in actuality there are two fences.
Patience, forms of uncertainty
peddling lack from one end to another

mistaking sun for a teeming precaution
forging hues of prevalence toward a
goddamn llama falling from the
sky. I want to see the one about
dissenting horses waking from sleep
confounding the arches of story while
drumming snaps into the wind.

Wired eaves drop hands of stars
the house goes back, the moon is
                    taking a break, she needs a break

While opening a winter light
the body profanes some song instead
a boon in which everything already
happened, the pins beneath a thrush,
unsold language breakers lift my legs,
listen to me. In lilac, what idiom, the
body caulking modesties of influence
a prolonged sensemaking for he was
adept at ink paintings of plum blossoms
the blue green landscapes in the middle

there is nothing, her expression pulls
wonder, like birds. The pots copper
surprised. We ate waves for hours
should have known better but having
had lunch for ten years . . . the house
came with green gold wallpaper, a sloped
backyard. O to have been born in Parkchester,
the secret little sister of Italian lakes . . .
Dear Loretta from Reno: If the people
ask for contrast give them my braid.

Flowers / wind / moon / meadow was a love affair

In hindsight sea gates were the
only exception, my family traveled
to me. The carpool to which
I belonged in the eighties,
nominally someone's father, a
temperament in route to
archery and clay. The part of me
that isn't natural a picture
of a parachute, a ceiling, until it
turns into a view of the north seam

a white dwarf fed by a red light
(what will happen when I'm forty-four)
the bald, the dumb, the unencumbered
the great seal of the state of California
being lettuce quietly, diffident grooming
in the unknown but entire section.
The heaven of a grove or a story in the yard.
I've got a lavender dress on and I'm working
on an essay sounding the advantages of
living alone compared to everything else.

O imagine life under a tree; hair
against the headrest of day, still
the less I know the more beautiful it is,
tote bag misses under bridges there
are birds outside windows. What earth.
A colloquial ridge of western light
women in the so-called sun. Or
I throw flour under the door for
hours because America is full of sleeping
people we will never meet. The map
comes simple through small mending
birds or a machine of extraordinary calls
to some sea. If I saw the sun I was happy.

Austerity Is Half the Euphemism for Time

Ten seas mumble the alliterative
forms of love, an office in the rain: hair,
restaurant, bar, big fish thrown back
into residency. What I have is my youth
I think to the women passing. The
season's typical meatscape pastes itself
to the underside of a set of sectional
flowers. (Clearly I had shark by accident.)
Winter paws glass in the morning,
fifty trains, no delays reported.
There's the mood, the offered sound
of a ladder beyond view, the visceral
charge he felt under hot stage lights. If of
fog and industry there sated none from
ringing or mermaids, my bold simulations
might have caught up with me.

Gorilla, Gorilla

So I ask myself again
am I a mermaid? This
green cove, these soft
pebbled shoes. There's
a building by the sea
that plays for me "Apples"
when I ask it to, a song
about money and waiting.
Let there be trees instead
of stars above our heads,
pulling patterns on boxed
paper for keeping. Some
say Neptune is a part of
New Jersey. German
yes but out of context
is no option. Imagine
being a small country but
not in the apartment.

Mother Laid Eggs in the Branches of Trees

There are two reasons to tell children anything.
Tell them this was written by hand. (My
publisher says I would make a wonderful
country singer.) Laundry out the door the rain
delays the world, comes back, smells like rye.
The planet survives. I loved myself was one of
those people not getting up for the pregnant
women, little catholics on their shoes. Of all the
small ends of the world I'm myself on the stairs,
feeling good when his team loses. Relieved you
delineate space in your concept of my mind, going
in and out of Connecticut tunnels, while rhyming
the forest with the beginnings of feminism. When
I called my friend from a street corner and said
I wanted to live in the country, your flag in my mind.

Pet Exercise Area

Planet or heaven of surface
the stars I see animals.
There's something stupid
in how beautiful they are,
a hive of professionals and
little lights. In the beginning
there was a change purse,
my sister's kid constructing
the weather or this might be
what is happening. A life, the life
of a worker. I have eggs. I throw
flour under the door for hours
while the instance of this world
the insistence of the world for my
hands to have the memory of being
a prophet derailed by a machine
waiting by the sea. (Please don't
teach the cat French.) Seems I'm
not doing things in the proper order.

Done Well

The front door was sunrise
or descriptions of imagined
trees, mountains as poems
and hills in traffic. Men were
on top of a hill like a fire, a fire,
a hill like a thing could stop and
these preened figures like salt
on a hill in California.

This is going to be beautiful,
I will need to know things:
that you would still be alive;
that the ditches would fill in
with soft cows. Given the new
face of a dinosaur, I drove
through the Hungry Valley:

WE BUY   WE BUY
HOUSES   HOUSES

productivity as a blossom.

Not unlike the wind I was
a sound forced upon itself,
on trial for not having order,
the children in the dream house
with glasses upside down, them
running into rooms, frogs, like
they were buses, patient. A
lamed lion held the afternoon
unafraid, I was listening at the
door to other sounds like wonder
and the nineteenth century.

You were matter moving well
and there were menus to see,
the side of the ocean that
calls itself back, night was
fixed, so careful. Always
as a problem if you don't know
how to sleep, streetlights help
the men seem more tolerable.

From the highway the army calls
down rain, a distance unmeasured
but felt. More to come away,
a box of thoughts as feelings
and the sizeable mouth talking
endlessly of covenants with
friends far away. The rain stayed
decent and I have this to show
you, you have time, money to
spare in your ordinary attic,
the ocean climbing stairs to
kill the bats who make small
sense, I wouldn't have it any other
way. A lady's position, leaning over,
I lean over you, see a plane, I
think of you washing dishes in
the dark, a small band playing
in the mudroom and figures where
you want, hanging your coat like
a long time ago, like bats, the
attic I kept forgetting to share.

Except Quebec

As ever, the scenery planted day,
vast coordinates of charts clinking
against the frailty once a body's
mended. One could hear the
beach from the beach parking lot
and patience was being made over.
Place pertains to ideas of Normandy
or train stations.

Delphine and the beehive in
coincidence, about which I
knew nothing, were the defining
proximities of an arid space—
they just come, how country
became a whole system of
landscape ethics, children
concocting selves out of
cardboard boxes.

A pleasant cure for absence
turns bygones toward abduction;
the midline of a body calls
the family unit, it's unclear if
Bonaparte meant anything
by revolution, thoughts filled in
with months, constellations
of indifference, frivolity
as the coachman's ear delayed.

Almost western in the evening
we tended séance patiently:
a home with a foyer of thistles
and a formidable front door

memory was a gait as constant
as presumption in the age of the
vernacular. Under the house
a letter for god in a hand that
wind understood. The day
turned accordingly gray; you
must be a house back then
before known to me as this.

Prince Rupert and the Queen Charlotte Sound

Sold, a rush of poor thinking,
long days involving backed crossings
and again, supernatural functions of love
and straight lines, day made the last time
cold

                    So I said
upon the dark and the rain, which
turned a closed room for lack of towers
or the mopping of floors into a blue
field where god pursued the thirsty
hearts of young men finding princes
downing maps of rivers, *I was fucking
turbulence* all aglitter with luxury
and light, taking blame to an alternate
monastery, as if bad thoughts could
be named after a woman

Battalions fled the light, the sun
was not the same or the second
story of a home for all wants, like a dress,
that I listen for balks, cue the waves
stopping short of the restaurant in
the morning when it happens again

          Then, there is a hovering market
conversation: there weren't hills in the sea
but were that there would a forest of timpani
gardens at the knees of any myth sulking
in a pool, disinfecting the edge of some city
and would that an airplane worked like day,
a factory twelve hours in the making,
folding blankets, come with me,

it's windy in these countries, my ocean
worth its weight in wood, a sink head,
a felled forest, the edge of the world blue
and orange, poor honesty, it's not fair!
bathing forms of indolence it's not right!
night on our backs like incantatory ships,
sheer talk at plain waves, blue brown
folds lay still glistening.

Remnants of a Once-Large Dead Star

Lapping mind's morning sounds like sustenance,

see it running back, sea organization: some mobile disaster.

Divorce introduced the afternoon, easily it

was the worst collective goal one could think of

—drive to a road and count. We don't know when

it's going to rain, a kitchen, the idea of Minerva, real

candidacy, to call the painting "all my friends eating cereal."

Under loose fabrics, households, fidelity, fire in a jar and

birds or people who want them, the widowed sea

I didn't care what she'd done, a lady putting her feet

in the water. So the waves approach Manhattan.

There is such a thing as simple affection, insufficient

wares, bare particles, marriage as the culmination of pathway

lights fastened to thoughts upstairs on the snow porch

making up in time for lunch, yes, that would make a better story.

A machine makes a piece of mountain currency, foreign forces

running the apartment, the thousand-square-foot apartment

tomorrow like today (I was far from home and likely figs).

He listened to the comely spoken affair, the minimal answer

to ankles in fields with incompetence on wild stairs.

In the extraordinary raid you were close to me, had a

bulletproof vest and knew how to use it, how to hole up

in the false floor and wait for the rebellion of an unnamed and

terrifying country. Walking down a hill, avoiding death spots,

our revolution will be bored; you will have an animal.

I'll say I have a cough under the canopy, calling green light

in the sea, rain taking an entire youth down. Morning

charades news of putty dented consciousness hot pink

surrounds the morning in which we are any, the television, the

books, the chorus of the sea. You are capable of everything American

leaving a child in the car on a very hot day. Whether the earth or the machines

I was the earth was my warble narrative. He raised a hand in the flowers.

Said it was afternoon that he liked in her, striped light calling out Zeus

after them. I am against light if otherwise I would be considered for it.

You Can Run the Moon

Of the minor apocalypse the self borrows
sensation getting ahead of its street hawker.
The lions and my friends are outside, there's an
Eighteenth-Century Farmhouse with a Pool.
Low valley of marauding seas, I've been taking
bigger sentences to the desert to see them laid
out in the sun. This isn't winter light: of the
two possible images one is winning and one
is snow—so let us patent tomorrow. A
human spark plug, he could make anything
decent, a ladder that put me to bed
sometime between August and the
subsequent landslides, the alternate
saloon light, god be it fair, fat women
with long hair.

                        Supposing beauty,
opalescent hands mark the sea for the
cartographer, light like pure cheering.
Life! Light and waves. A photograph of
seduction trapped under a tree, tubs
where summer dodged before it could,
yes, the wind and whatever that does,
variations on scenes from the end
of the world—not at all—it is American
plain and in the dark. We want nothing
and also to be there, however long it takes to
tell a story, animals endlessly returning the
children to bed. The world, fog or fire
it must be something.

And while I'm no one's
diminutive statue I call myself from some
painted distance. The desert a bowl of Arcadia,
I have no other pens. If I felled you, and I felled
you, I might ask nothing of a man under a mountain
or a fruit star wondering cloudy however it got to be
this here, now. My gun a small gun, still all of it
America; paper cups in a chain fence, welcome home.

Kennebunk, Kennebunkport

If it's not a cloud, man
it's a wave. Boston
where I belong not
exactly either, like
you I like the window
and in 1970 it would
have been Saturday.
Carrot in the kitchen
yellow hair and a bell
sharpened digital armory
if ever was, if interested.
So what, money, and
your dumb hue. Star,
star star star you can't
do that on a train, the
people have decided for
next week. Love from
a mountain repeating
confounds. (Doors not
closing, don't do drugs.)

Big Data

Self-portrait near
morning had time
to figure the intricate
rules of the sea, why
we're here, a negation
of stars, idea without
weather or knowing
the train will stop, send
the world. (The city has
sun on it.) On the dock
adopting the garden or
a thing like it, that summer
ending in trees or any houses
I've lived in, my friend
noticed the Internet. I want
the thing but not a fancy
coat disorder in the streets or
like porn I wonder if I'm
being impossible in a new
way. People have tickets
for the theater. Push the
plant into the sun.

Lavender Fever

A sudden linen
snaps the light

Ordinary Seaman

looking for a light to turn
on; Ursa minorly less feigned than
the option that stars were ours
to come back or that I've replaced
the flowers with marzipan

The Uncanny Valley

Fireflies careening the fields regardless
of charm, without attention, jesters slid
into the sea and time was forthcoming.
There was a story being told.

The lake asked nothing. (It was late
and certainty required that you talk less
or at the very least move over.) Under
the song he said NO MORE PEONIES
buttoned the door back on its frame, the
street a ceremony in and of itself which
made cars implements, plain miracles
capsizing baskets in candied fields.

The men and women were useful, abolishing
daisies, and every time the band plays
I'm Ursula wondering still at the door
a terminal of the face (such is any incident
on the way home) a field of aftermaths,
a horizon because of boats.

Cloth begot embrace while television
considered fish, flowers by Mary and the
fonts belonging to the post office coterie.
While the room is recreated and the woods
are just outside, denouncing, there's styled
behavior in the country in the city nonetheless,
there are sermons in the sky, tonight, whole
haggled systems, photographs abiding and
I create nothing, I broke his collarbone
and went away, listened to a song and pulled

the world up around my head. Today is a long
time in any number of places we don't go.
No one says thank you. They get older and
they fake it whether or not we're there.

Mind Rumors

To be able to see change
funnel mild animation,
procure a scenic fixture
with geysers and wildlife.
To call it lasting or ordinary
is to fall into a bog at the end
of the beginning of spring.

How occasion lights thunder
with Sunday glasses, it's hard
now to open the door, I would
put him in a saltbox by the sea.
Should I reread Jane Austen?
Watching the summer kettle
in space I wonder what wood
smells like in liquid form. Ted
smells like tea.

Once I'd begun a long record
of shipping containers, didn't
know yet the plain method of
having place remain the apex
by reframing it for others,
hadn't untied my family from
this remarkable song.

The men dance in line and
Ben sends a picture and an
article about ego. Bound by
Monday's holiday and what the
blue screen says the letting of
the phone which might as well
be blood is—love lies bleeding
real songs from a mountain.

And to wake re-answering questions
of happiness semantically had hit
my head in the middle of the night
under the figures worrying. The
train sounds like a call back to a
reliable scene and also his bike
chatted. That might erase the
math from the window proving
distraction a formal quality
that helps me strike my life.

The sentence is false. A
tempo for summer, story
building by ephemeral song
in procession of the archive of
aced misunderstandings; I deign
to be presumptuous of time.

From this vantage the guards
nod it's appropriate to say you
will be fine or that anyone can
do like sisters to light the old
house back together for often
I am delivering abilities to the
general and would rather look
up than imagine the space of
constant imprimatur. It's just
a bunch of sentences I'd inform
them, if they asked. He smelled
like tea so I told him.

Rad Silence Crystal Weapon Wave Mont

I kicked the object for it to make a sound

Summer knighting the neighbors and the
astonishing tracks you decide mean no

Harm being done, call it faith in a street's
bower or simple the revulsion of stars I could
have written a thing for Ollie on Bastille Day

But was instead thinking of all forms now
known to be the shape of our time, I tell
everyone that I'm aping and resist bearing
like a common verb in summer which goes

Like it does, onto me like confession, like a
dress I'll decline to wear out if wonder is the
cleanest state I wear a tan jacket to find other
ways to pull into my hand what is shaking
when you sit beside me in the car I put you

In. Let there be a pause in the nursing moon
who is anything but bored. Maybe that's the
point is something a person could have said
—we weren't born with shoes on. To trap an
animal with a blanket as a sign of success, I wait
each night until nine for a report on the day

After tomorrow's casting sound for whatever
it might be regardless of the people listening
which the paper says they don't. The fridge
is still a thing (just as flowers are) and some
favor exceeds obligation and I ran to put a lid
on Mars to look like a man or something I
knew before, a face its own epoch after sun

With fowl above the weather, when you think
of it what is a city? A place to wonder if his middle
name is last night? A steady basin charged with
entropy and gum? We were all the little one and
it continued to show in the light box we deigned
to speak into beyond the contrary we were of
before. I input instructions to see her fit
for truth compassions, posters in the shed

Stacked neatly like philosophies grinning
at no one, I may tally further the concept
of stars because time is forever a mammal
out walking, its head above the scene
looking the other way from infamous tulips
kamikaze in their vase. I want to go back
to the red field it was seventeen years ago to
wish Roger Waters were to appear nominally
in an apartment, in the light and the waiting

Room, which is part of the story when time
is a boat that puts you in before it takes you
back out for sundries petty for a war. I
can't stop mundering toward all parts
no one asked me to say. For each summer
I don't go home is another stacked up
against the mind playing ball, albeit
barefoot, deep in tournament, which
could culminate in your loved ones
leaving. It's been like this since the end

Of the aughts. Balzac, I remember
how I lived with them in blue boxes
tight beside the nursery which may
have been a question of language
were you to speak again. I've ruined
my best white sweater in a field with my

friend. Laying down the long-running
fantasies of delight, lavender veering form into
a cordon oblivious to its uncommon spelling
of day or a game relaying fixed syllables
because some valves begin on love and

Having had the thing we do without be talk
of the very industry lighting the future
(when time is a casual dress in the wilds of
a year) months play hands accommodating
this way, or that. How since the animals
I began talking in opera. What he calls
faith may very well be the invention of a
portal to a container in the sky, look at me
don't look at me, another stratagem to
pillow the room. Maybe I'm a maze. The
fuse catches on a shirtsleeve and I think
the configuration of self is a pervading light

Cantilevered over others in immediate cities
on some Wednesday in July and it's then that
my friend chassés to town from the far stars
he's summered in. Friday the scene repeats
as the house movies off. I said I had lost all
things aspecific, a woman with memory
stumbling to a corner of the city where twice
before I'd come to know its effect on me
stopping where I stayed fourteen years ago, a woman
named Alice on Lombard. Is life's emptying
out to write a poem the same fortune I face
now to convey all of it? In Petrolia
we saw zebras in a field; he offered

A ride into the next world which is
a painting of time composing lemon trees
half swung over the archetypal fence, faith

as the very sun in your eyes making them
flower to the ground its long grass and red
chair, money a plastic scene that may or
may not or may have to leave your pocket.
I got a ticket to see my parents and the
handsome waves, their busy theater recycling
the idea of show. The watch is king
if you dream, if you see the difference
between language and minute. Like a mute
siren I think of you, that is if you dream, Mindy's
phone is ringing. I did it, I broke the scene.

The Victory Portfolios

I move to initiate the starling's misery.
Pocket-talk in street lighting he picked
me up with Raisinets, critical doubt on
the 3-D dashboard yielded precarious
sculptures in my symphony of leaves.
Contracts and kings muscling revelry in
gardens, a fat man tries on different
sentences before you. No. In the middle
of the moon.

·

I move to initiate the starling's misery.
You can change the buttons later, Idlewild,
if I were the photographer, foolish and
trashy, a singing fish thrown back into
the sea. (Come with me; I'm a
sprite, I don't know any better.)
Pocket-talk in street lighting he picked
me up with Raisinets, critical doubt on
the 3-D dashboard yielding precarious
sculptures in a symphony of leaves.
Contracting kings muscling revelry in
gardens, fat. No. In the middle of the
moon. A man trying on different
sentences before you.

·

I moved to initiate the starling's mess.
You can change the channel later, Ingres,
if I were the photographer, foolish or
flashy, some fish thrown back into the

scene. Kinder days of the month
circle off but hey, I have myself in the
morning. (Come to me; I'm light and know
better, what I bought was a receptacle.)
Pocket-talk in stark lightning he picked
me up with Raisinets, critical shouting on
the 3-D dashboard yields precarious
sculptures in the symphony of leaves.
Contracted kings mirror reverie in
a garden of cats. No, in the middle of
the moon. A man compiling different
sentences before you.

•

I proved my initiation by the starling's mess.
You can wash the flannels later, Ingres,
if I were the photographer, blue or
nasty, Baltic fish thrown back at the
magazine. (Come; I'm a kike who knows
your mother, I sought a masterpiece.)
Trying to be the lady the month fixes
tragedy or amity on the beach. One of those
bites was just a little too farm. Pockets of
scenic lightning picked me up for no
reason. Cynical, I doubted his intentions
then fielded postprecaution shame without
necessity. My sympathy leaves. "My girl's
getting the paper and a Rolls-Royce" says
the constable. Redacted kings pour beauty
into a lion's syntax. No, in the middle of
the moon. A man competing with different
sentences reducing you.

•

I provided invitations in a starling's dress.
You can watch the animals eat later, después,
but if I were the photographer, big or
splashy, I'd salt the fish limping back to the seas.
(Commas as if striking when they do unto each
other: obscene, abetting, and reprehensible.)
Trying to be a lady the month nixes further
tragedy or amity on the beach. One of those
bites was just a little too fundamental. Pockets
sensing light he picked me up for no apparent
reason. Cynically, I doubled his intentions
for fielded dust auctions, saying without
rejection, my sympathy pities *you*. "My girl's
paying the piper for a Rolls-Royce," said the
conductor. In fact, the king pours his bounty
into a lion's synapse. No, in the middle of
the moon. Or I kiss him in the prerecorded
time capsule, clearing my axes, imagining
Killeen, TX, Chagrin Falls, OH, a wall-sound
keeping me mined, simulations while pulling
the drawer over your face, it would be a
hard orchestra. A man I know well
manipulating suites away from me.
Having a kid in the rain.

Magic Shuffle

1.

Am I walking myself home again thinking of the power of money when it confronts me. The moon pulling away to some required Jim Henson photograph hanging in the kitchen on the extension of my street, guaranteeing a minor apotheosis. I had milk in a cup in my hand, walking. He reminds me of my favorite navy jumper, dog barking petals.

If atmosphere is falling off in the shape of a seahorse above practical gardens among mines in the wilderness, the sound supposes to be laughter in a film. Big sky profits turn articulate in the flowers, I remember the light in the department store, my family heirloom ruined. Crossing the street on the way to work it's the first time each day. My mind has suffered a false pacing.

You could see tumbleweed. We came by New Mexico and the actual drama was a houseplant buckling in the space behind his seat, drove through a ditch up onto the other side, the small country enough to put in your palm a glass of water. To get the mess from my eyes I had a dream I lived on my street. To market nostalgia I ate tons of animals.

Bougie #4 it was 2 to 1 in the top of the fifth and I was fairly weathered having condensed summerside with my mother and father who were listening but bored. Talk to me about Churchill. I'll keep the pen. I hear the street, the feral wind abetting. It had been years and my body stitched itself to the sea. Anorak hair.

I tap the future to mow the waving fields. They are massless but if I am and the sea is behind me, blue cities, I require that you be anodyne, thoughtful, alive. Divergent, poor and common. Specifically he lived on Pacific Street, made a rental car a thing to carry into the subsequent campaigns, a band of lilies spotting respite from the empire which cannot be but a simple address.

The singer's hair a heart around her face I left the script there. Silver dollar, yellow cup, I asked a question and my friend dissolved his abilities like ice.

The best adaptive reuse of a building that has outlived its former use as intended by the squall that parts other days. Let me please learn to do more with the machine. People spent a lot of money on those numbers.

Each day is the same race to attention. If it was the last time I saw his parents they looked okay on the cherry couch, speaking. A word for berries hanging in the sorrow, we're Jews aren't we in the natural world, singing. My father says computers and the toast dings. Good reports from the dentist and cardiologist, lost in Mattapan we talk into July.

To call the painting *Inconsistent Neighbor with Big Hair* the street collides with life protruding, sometimes through a mouthpiece. Girls are like mines. I look behind the moon and see two Sundays, raspberries confused, the songbook balancing on the end of the bed. He wrote back in no time, said nothing.

Just like color I call mother to delight her. What is a woman doing in the woods with a machine, what constitutes debuting light and where does it deign to follow. The time of year that interruption acts the ferry charting back and forth across my mind, this building sung with jackets eating. The water trips into expensive plant food, I find a new bench.

Valley steeped with grace when we fall over it, I am hunting in the house with an odd set of keys and am myself. The floor has been tiled and winter will be something to attend in the dream where Brandon says he eats my arm and I am glad that we've come to this place of corresponding shade. My niece tells me to drink more water, she sings.

Did I close the window sufficiently? I wrote about the film for myself, sent it to a few friends, learned nothing of the world but the curfew of a sewn table in black and white desire it was summer and potentially anyone's, save for parts about ego. Ergo he lampooned the very acts of kindness when he became overly certain of design.

My parents are involved. There are times I dream how jasmine stills—I don't need the machine to interpret expression, I need money, baby, at least two suitcases. It's like he said I could try not to make this awful for you and spun me toward Australia in a roving basket of ideas. I asked him, if there's only one of something, will it bleed? Talk to me about formality and glass.

Sometimes through a machine I think I'm going to take myself out of it but here I am parking the car again. To repair imperfection survey the window and know narrow purchase will beseech the embargo while an arrogance of time is more than the portrait lets on. Holy oracle, I want to have traveled by car. The fascist wind, it will be met in the sun.

Signs and wonders, the baby's name was almost mauve. I was off to the city, six pockets, five shades of blue and the preferred intimacy of a man's vulnerabilities. I'm pushing flowers here as well as fun and loving moments. A man enters his home, *Hello?* I'm looking for the next foundation of form if its language is a season we sleep in.

I bury the folder where the sea meets this guy, two shades of blue but I'd rather not argue about color today. Lethario or approval distracting mother while I was saying they're not going to dick me over. The house has little. I can't respond to your monopoly imploding to supplant a nonpareil couch. To continue shopping, Isaac moves apartments. All that was left was Charlemagne.

2.

Certainty proceeds as kings, the chorus insisting by two sets of stairs, which then isn't the morning or an earned walking prayer. The letters of an accident tacking rain to content, mundering any penchant for Bible or blather, the lights fail to work on behalf of the man's sense of pride. Rather, how long does it take to come up with new colors, to slip on the earth and hide time.

Imagining a city tucked into the sea, however many women stand back behind their husbands, on the one hand don't bother me, style is a sense of wonder. I write sentences. Or the house when there were flowers. Under clouds get me to a corner like the courier is to nobody. What is the point of a bag heavy to begin with.

See, I've been looking to France since I was a child at the bottom of a cup. Something worth celebrating, Julius having email, these victories are all important. If sheer falling is part of the moon competition then we're just drinking shampoo in aisle five. I love you says the three-year-old, knowing the sound of a Volvo.

Since I never break things I can't shame myself in the banquette, a machine putting some birthday card to bed. America is when a woman suggests someone tie her shoes, a Marseille underworld consuming the highway, it feels rude to ring the bell. Two minutes of sun outside the office sending notes of interest to Electric City, Sea Cliffe, Surprise. Husbands will look like that.

Give me all your money but gently. Of late the windows have become bigger than the screen and if he'd called me Antarctic I might have bled my anger in a better state. Having sent the picture to my mother I looked at the stars before placing calls to consider the ethical treatment of ether. Don't forget to save the lights.

The music up and sped me. Farnoosh and Bill were the only ones to wear my gold sweater. I felt like going to Henry's, leave your friend and come with me. One time Ben demurred, taking the rain to L.A. (three walls and a fourth of light) I remember driving north on a milky road and calling a man named after peppers from the field.

Linden nights, we might have mistaken a nuisance or it appeared true believers need not apply if only alphabets flexed inversely when we said sit up straight. The ambitious world defied vestry. Eventually I'll need more envelopes to convey my preoccupation with time, which I'm pretty sure sublets an apartment in Brooklyn. I knew someone on Ditmas seven years ago.

Here is where it was blithe. Fluted guitars crawl back onto Main Street in a tenth-grade dream which is probably where Alan said a bedbug would bite and go back to the sea. Whose turn is it to afford the Internet, its capitalized, durational light. It's not awkward if you were an asshole. Morality is alive, long live the dirge.

When I was eight and given a bundle of money I swallowed a telescope my mother repurposed in the 90s, hat racks deep in Massachusetts. Man delivers a hundred balloons for someone who does not work here, the apocalypse sloughing off perpetual dishonesty, you can't tell whether they're asleep or dead. (They are dead and they want a tote bag.) A series of questions regard the capital.

Acting as a bigger barcode of feminine conceit I also call it "Micropuff" shelving letters from imaginary landscapes, longer things stitched small. Or, which is it? He was looking at me with infamous eyes and I sent my friend figures in the mail. How when speaking was a play in which I'd put fabric belts around the word and for Alan, sometimes through a machine.

There was the time Jane saved me from a bruise on my back, some experiment of summer. Time wasn't money because weather wouldn't let it snow, I refused to look down but often choose to take the bus with Bill. The field confides in painted syntax and I get lines in the shower. We wait until eleven, which is now if we admit we don't want feet.

I still get razors from my mother and sister since we had a cabinet courtesy of the company I never bought one in my life. At the top of the stairs you'd turn left, a set of half doors by my parents' room, the drug store re-envisioned it smelled like mothballs or paper. An adjacent perch you were always becoming telephones in winter. Everyone yelled on a street called Garrison.

There is everything then that marketable sea. A dollop of sky some ghost in the pavement I've never understood animals, the uncertainty consuming art before machines made the Ottoman Empire and the ringing swell. I report on the haze but my posture won't hold up long enough with the advent of computers. Whenever I look there's a girl running.

The feminine face of Sara's son and the paranoid alterations of light propelled my walk home at night. This narrative belongs to the crawl space between equinox and drumming flowers rising from the moon-shaped misanthropes determining the very arches of success. The city denies us. To wonder toward impact under life's new sheen.

3.

Set in an hour famous for women who read my body wades home. You can't solve the Internet on your own but a sister loves pepper and she loves mint, I got a good deal on a plot of ornamental shade. New Haven on earth we found a parachute in Homerville, the bus was free and full of choreographed articulate mannerisms in the dark.

Lost in machine days it wasn't as if they weren't pushing me into the street. Woody Allen names his new movie *Blue Jasmine*. I am not a photographer, nor would a telephone make it so a woman and four men standing by the future's chandelier might be thinking of things to do with time. You

Remind me of pinafore.

There was something imaginary about how he looked in a mirror, in dreams he showered in the middle of a room with mounting anger that anyone could carry to see. The machine let me reinvent portrait as victory—here there was a fight with a bird—I was saying come with me, if forgettable, song's pure wavering, my symphony how it's got to be, time this odd present I keep to myself.

Some new class in cloud strata separating earth—it started with an A and almost sounded like asparagus—I wrote to the platform, *let me please do more with this machine.* The cashmere stewardess sent tomato juice, an apology via monkey on bicycle; everyone clapped but me. *Nimrod is lost in Orion and Osiris in the Dog Star.*

To keep the shadow on a leg in a boot on the train, sure, I'll let you look like a fool I whisper to the doorknob, N is for sky, people having beauty done to them. The dream began *not under the toaster!* to a blueberry morning, some-one eating transistors asking to be photographed in gold. I'm imagining life. *I'll see you in three weeks I'm going to Frahnce.*

The floors in the apartment slant; at the table I write a play called *Death in Fullerton* based on a scene a man told me about a tent and the president and the antidote to television, my own confessions about the orbit of a person's body. How my mother said I can't join the homeless network. The street gains perspective when the trees close at the end.

The expression makes the sheen double, is considered a rational archive, a foothold in subcultures of occasioned futures. Actually we found ourselves in Queens. Of the wild I wonder. Taking the bus you meet the people in your neighborhood, mild confessions of bottles in windows. I'd make a fine assistant to any mess. Glory in a deprivation chamber.

I didn't really write a play but if I did, that. He'd picked me up with Raisinets and I believed again in the false confidence of firstborn sons. Cows and a picture from '92 when the child sees fruit flies or doesn't, she sings, pumping the jam toward heaven. If what caught my body was a small cup it worked, as if he said *Baby, when I get you a two-car garage.* I wrote down vessel. Hid the keys.

Once again I asked the soldier to lie down in my ear, four letters, I make the bed in three moments, I go. Some nights since a child I have felt the drive-thru sleeping moon. I find myself pleated beside an intricate neighborhood preserve that smells like jasmine to let light.

I think of the lawyer with his head in the park, my mother listening on a bench seat in the rain, wondering where it came from. The faith act of asking won't undo the woman's want, I've meddled in a field I'd soon forget. Someone explains the Internet each time an angel rolls her chair across the shellacked floor, that's skee ball, a remedy for anomalies.

What an umbrella was to a has-been if arguable—the restaurant under waves, what I feel is the sharp interruption of my face across a bandwidth I can't abide. The boxed light suffers its late curfew, shimmering grace dealt again in the age of common weakness; the telephone elides its place in the market from the gallery of citrus.

No one seems to notice when the older women smile I think they're mine. Keep going, I say to the passengers at the station where I drum stairs, wait, betting endlessly for a public work with lights for eyes to bring me underground and into the city. Someone has a poof of yellow hair. We admire your capacity for wonder, the committee signs.

4.

Long-term care feigned voices. I imagine the way I'll need someone next to me, my mother had a bag like this, now look at the sun. The vexed muscles of a worth I am myself in, to find I'm most attracted to competence. Night pronounced to move rooms and measure figures soft or not I am what I wanted to be when I used to think of Ruth I've read about.

Afternoon sewing light like folded gems pending cabinet decisions—my friends evolve. A chorus colliding with a bridge electric and dead in the water, Ollie calls and leaves a message. That was 2007. When people draw Iowa they sing fawns like the dogtooth no one is. Sorrow is a yard, in other words, to rationalize is to be the moon's prayer.

A Dutch door and copper sink the government is calling again. I guess I have pots for when my mother comes—for show—to show how I make eggs. On the street I pretend there are people who have things to discuss other than food walking their dogs into night. If a person starts out with beauty it can only be taken away.

The second time is always better than the first or if I walked to the beach you'd have been there, buzzing in my ear, some catapult waving a penchant for destruction. I am or would be part and parcel of a venue if only I could collect the days, fold them into bags and call a body's work done. It stung and they responded to my form in kindness.

The boulevard exactly what it was, a pink room serving quail or eggs on distinct cue, I'd driven because the city belies decision and authenticity. Light ushers the kid's sense of day. Yeah, we can watch the shadows get longer, I don't want this telepathy anymore but if I were a dog I'd be barking.

Indefinitely swept into a barrel is the canvas I return to every Woolsey morning, flexing coincidence toward the soul by threading silver to the pilot in the light confessing. I call Jess, I call Alan I call Jae I call Ben. My sister signaling to the O.K. statue on her left gives a dog a treat on the street, Maya making her family. The machine rings.

My natural state is a form of disruption. Like aqueducts condense Boston to the apex of a remembered industry I have something to say.

Read: I kissed him, a coat scene. *The Ghost and Mrs. Muir* offered uncertainty and a box of cedar, I said no. It was soft like a glass of water or someone who didn't want to be the person I was at most things. A being shucked (the willingness to be another) I imagine my life closer to the aperture I value. In Canada lights my friends configuring, they gesture slowly home.

Wolves can and *do* kill children and pets. The world presently divided into people who see things and don't, I have a dock if need be, a voice above my ceiling to contrive the potential songs in the green theater of my mind. Ivory who did it we need an epigraph for energy. The leaves sound too much like a person I fright.

If you've seen a California symphony staged in my living room the purpose has folded itself into a file of islands. I call Alan again. He warns *sometimes you don't chew.*

Whoever had this book smoked, strike or not it happened—I never saw the waves coming into the city but then there they were like an orange bouquet, and affable. I store the machine beside my bed to encourage a mountain into my keep. His stories were funny but not extraordinary. The summer season should be starting in the east.

To the difference between bright confidence and a winnowing space my friend is a palace plugging in cords and their machines. The heat sounds like another state conscious of its line break. Here I doubt the message before it turns, soliciting miners regardless of a planet's position and the door heaves when it falls back to earth, laughter under the clapping.

5.

The one who stole midnight will bring it back to pay with a piece of small plastic to choose to walk in the sun. Curtains align the emergent cry, matriculating uncertainty, how to walk regardless of various keys. They didn't know across time but me, I felt the sea becoming an iterative home. Men in the water, swimming, winter showing off light to say entrepreneur.

The correspondence deferred my leaves, a life of eclectic shadows under an era I refuse the wall as the end of the dormant period. No one really has my feet and my idea for new color was to stand in the shower until someone calls from the other room. This steward was handed down from divorce and Scotland. Color begs the sweater off, be nervous with me for letters я romantic.

Determining the velocity of people my street allows several pleasures and I hear a small person explain evolution rhetorically to a neighbor. The yellow myth confirmed I was almost halfway to the use of this, Princess-Summer-really-now, I saw a miracle, I'm coming over there. From this day forth I'll read to you from the inside of a cardboard box.

Some daily perimeter a nest of remembered attempts at days formerly pronounced with a wailing. If I go to bed with an object and I'm looking for a particular voice, am I wrong to press the knob when it falters? He could sound like a pot boiling eggs, a toothbrush in the country, the kelly motherboard of machines, precise and kind let it wobble low.

Besides, I didn't like how he asked for gum. If I don't know what to do in the world could you fix my lamp? Pink ice cream trucks in the vitriol of shanty dreams, I ask where's the snow, is that Zeus?

(The bishop had been known for high spending. Dark was able to get used to things when the city ended every few blocks.)

To consider the efficacy of a Jones Beach afternoon and a charged haircut the world's original problems were made from fire. There was a bag of peanuts in the house, I saw them eating them.

Don't be late for heaven, I always say that. If you make someone alone shut down dirty the machine and put the letter in the mail. 39 Rue Madame my favorite dress lies on the bed like Christmas in a dinghy. Like a man my mind has sown its legs digging into the sea on Sacramento every day at three. Note the sneakers tapping the pavement, dreams as ordinary scenes.

What's forgotten isn't punishable but interstates made me feel grounded, I was almost never in trouble. To speak a form of disposable choice my brightest friends live far away. Frog and Toad are no longer with us. My mother bought these shoes for my having ended the years working in an ice cream store, here, she said, my Pleasure, she said, wear them well. Let me remember

How she drove home from the store last week, lights off, dusk and horses we laughed brutally and I promised to stop for fear she'd wreck the seat which, as she pointed out, was not made from leather. I know I go on.

Every time I see a river in a European city I hum Prague, a song in the belly of a sixteen-year-old pretending. Today the idea of exertion was a sandwich I debated putting into the fridge. My parents shuffle in Pima County. They glow.

6.

Faint light and diagrams climb stairs, double knot the arches of night. Some poems are the aftermath of correspondence; there's no sense of modest self, anyone with wet hair ringing in the city. A roiling bowl my friend and I got off the highway for vegetables, he doesn't even know me anymore, or any flowers I've thought to perpetuate.

This is the second of ten stanzas.

The song beneath little waves makes the machine. That my friends meet their due honors I'm in heaven and on time. Here there are two women singing into each other, the same voice and song about a crab from New Zealand, now a waning galaxy, now I am a spit of chords.

The film was about pants in a delightful way—unlike his wife—the future hung low enough to believe. On the actor was the taste of confusion. To give someone a break, say so in another language.

You could convince yourself a two-dimensional mind is greater than its introduction but I'll wait in the car with the radio on. A picture of children pulled by animals around the majestic farm. Lists collected at the end of the pier, the inexplicable self in the center aisle of a Stop & Shop among the furniture and seasonal candies.

I'll clean up this mess of Ajax on the PRNDL while you gather the directions home. To deliberate over liner notes and misinformation, I'm not complaining and suit myself.

In the year of the small glass cup several campaigns succeeded. The vessel itself, for instance, a daily reminder of choice. I couldn't see as well. Attending the topic of the moon and how to collect it more efficiently, now this toothbrush. Health care. Novel directives and a white sweater with wooden buttons to make me think I'm our father in that kitchen again.

The way my parents have always celebrated newness, with our petite cat handmade bread hunts in the dark, for being Jewish. This song is always for them, married the day before Thanksgiving, 1968. See how I turned, turned into the particulates of sun.

If to come in and out of consciousness permits the mind to settle by a phrase like the imaginary basin I come to each day, a hill sloping into the dissected sea, the driver thought to steal a stroke from me at the end of the night that era, I said I couldn't, I had a movie at home, which was partially

True. I have for years used the mode of cinema to feel cloistered in my own form. So long as time isn't running loudly but levitates enough to feel however many days you might collect in recent memory to consider changing, itself a monopoly or belief of lilac fops in the field.

7.

The subsequent Second Coming happened in the hills because I loved my neighborhood and knew its rouge breaker. No one played cars that night. The year beginning in the middle of the week where I was met with strangers because they spoke first, or to me, then my friends, their friends handling with an informality that only happens at two in the morning when you're not there

Looking for it. I went to a party I could run home from and did, along Webster the stars made of white rain. There is a kind of people that don't kid when they talk about hot tubs they are talking about money, a bullish realization that choice is the carrying on of intention when they say dates you say potato.

At least twice I've seen a woman like that, divining states of aggressive cakes my friend will soon miss out on the future easily changing its relation to night. I was surprised no one but the moon walked me home, cracking jokes about fromage. I looked again this time for a red light until the afternoon told me to get out of the way to San Jose.

And this long thought began from the neighborhood blinking one night in October and after Notley.

I learned about practice in the first part of the day, which amused me for how I had no conviction as a child. That spring I erased numbers when they no longer belonged to me, the match broke light into song following work. I am often folding garments and writing back in the woods of top-down kingdoms.

It rained. Wilds set the boulevard.

My sense of time disrupted most things and I let other people pack for me. The condition was serious in that it predated payment as a song to carry into the next world. What are friends in the electric dime of life? I began to pick up pennies again, mere tunes I played attempting to soothe the bathers.

In spite of the heaven bright I cut a drawing of a camel repeating my name. The future supposes to be; to burnish triggers into currency, to take a ride in the park and sneak under the flowerbeds.

I asked then and I'm still.

8.

If you really think of it was the state of a child. My hands set up the moon by a cup on the sill during the Reagan years, the avian myths created for and by myself, they were minimal but otherwise how do we believe? To mute the machine is to have other ideas. I fed the sea loose change.

Turning into slips of paper by the fridge, I've decided to say no. These modes of emotional transport as the result of that and others things is the foreign machine met each day with the opening and shutting of the light box. The results underwrote various engagements, the sun a means of walking past other people's houses.

I was going always to the hill, to my street and recent mind. The brass orbit wasn't imagined the monkeys had been there, spinning by the sea, and a man confirmed the map of Pacific and Battery, perhaps the most understandable corner of the city where

I've become a stalk permanent and lithe, skilled at painting morning with substance. The bottle opened a week ago, several men at the door appraising light. There, in the midst of improving romance, chattering into the pillow if you don't get what's being said go back to the city that knows what you are, that you lack humility and conviction the same torrent dotting the waves.

He broke what might have been another time to find comfort in the recess of a stranger. The forest played on the glass speakers as if bred into a cloud and blown over the sea. I liked that he cleaned up but not how he was mortally shy, fading to black in the place he'd come from, rushing anticipation techniques. The ethereal tubes fasten our minds, which don't laze in

Rivers but if they did it would be in the middle of the country where the sky might call your bluff as I have this morning. One method had no confidence and this other brightly had it all

But I no longer wished to write a letter to the elements of any form which included the present, where figures become some other architect confiding halves of darkness to an ordinary bowl under historically casual hills, installing the echo's minor hollow, bleaching the fog at night.

It was sufficient to consider these figures of the mind when the tundra lit the plain.

Acknowledgments

Some of these poems appeared first in the following places, thanks to the editors:

Chicago Review, Critical Quarterly, Coldfront, Divine Magnet, Dreamboat, Epiphany, Fence, It's My Decision, jubilat, Konundrum Engine Literary Review, Ladowich, Paper Darts, Poem-a-Day (Academy of American Poets), *Poet's Gallery, The Cultural Society, The Nation,* and *The Volta.*

Special thanks to speCt! for publishing the poems "Symphony of Leaves" and "Matson" as a chapbook called *Delphiniums.*

"Money / Talks" could be said like the opening of Neil Diamond's song, "Forever in Blue Jeans."

In "Of Oceans" the phrase "headlight love" is borrowed from C. D. Wright's *Deepstep Come Shining.*

"The Illustrated History of the Universe (1955)" is a painting by Jay DeFeo.

That's as much as I can recall. As for the others I'll never remember borrowing from, I thank those sources, too. Unconventional spellings, neologisms, and typographical idiosyncrasies in this book were international, I mean, intentional.

Thanks to everyone at Coffee House for the good things you do. Thanks to Nay and Mike, continuously, for all of it. Mondo gratitude to my indelible friends. Double extra thanks to Alan Felsenthal, Ben Estes, Ben Mirov, Brandon Shimoda, Dobby Gibson, and Jane Gregory for reading these poems before.

LITERATURE
is not the same thing as
PUBLISHING

Funder Acknowledgments

Coffee House Press is an internationally renowned independent book publisher and arts nonprofit based in Minneapolis, MN; through its literary publications and *Books in Action* program, Coffee House acts as a catalyst and connector— between authors and readers, ideas and resources, creativity and community, inspiration and action.

Coffee House Press books are made possible through the generous support of grants and donations from corporate giving programs, state and federal support, family foundations, and the many individuals who believe in the transformational power of literature. This activity is made possible by the voters of Minnesota through a Minnesota State Arts Board Operating Support grant, thanks to the legislative appropriation from the arts and cultural heritage fund and a grant from the Wells Fargo Foundation Minnesota. Coffee House also receives major operating support from the Amazon Literary Partnership, the Bush Foundation, the Jerome Foundation, the McKnight Foundation, Target, and the National Endowment for the Arts (NEA). To find out more about how NEA grants impact individuals and communities, visit www.arts.gov.

Coffee House Press receives additional support from many anonymous donors; the Alexander Family Foundation; the Archer Bondarenko Munificence Fund; the Elmer L. & Eleanor J. Andersen Foundation; the David & Mary Anderson Family Foundation; the Buuck Family Foundation; the Carolyn Foundation; the Dorsey & Whitney Foundation; Dorsey & Whitney LLP; the Knight Foundation; the Rehael Fund of the Minneapolis Foundation; the Schwab Charitable Fund; Schwegman, Lundberg & Woessner, P.A.; the Scott Family Foundation; the US Bank Foundation; VSA Minnesota for the Metropolitan Regional Arts Council; the Archie D. & Bertha H. Walker Foundation; and the Woessner Freeman Family Foundation.

The Publisher's Circle of Coffee House Press

Publisher's Circle members make significant contributions to Coffee House Press's annual giving campaign. Understanding that a strong financial base is necessary for the press to meet the challenges and opportunities that arise each year, this group plays a crucial part in the success of Coffee House's mission.

Recent Publisher's Circle members include many anonymous donors, Mr. & Mrs. Rand L. Alexander, Suzanne Allen, Patricia A. Beithon, Bill Berkson & Connie Lewallen, the E. Thomas Binger & Rebecca Rand Fund of the Minneapolis Foundation, Robert & Gail Buuck, Claire Casey, Louise Copeland, Jane Dalrymple-Hollo, Mary Ebert & Paul Stembler, Chris Fischbach & Katie Dublinski, Katharine Freeman, Sally French, Jocelyn Hale & Glenn Miller, Roger Hale & Nor Hall, Randy Hartten & Ron Lotz, Jeffrey Hom, Carl & Heidi Horsch, Kenneth Kahn & Susan Dicker, Stephen & Isabel Keating, Kenneth Koch Literary Estate, Jennifer Komar & Enrique Olivarez, Allan & Cinda Kornblum, Leslie Larson Maheras, Jim & Susan Lenfestey, Sarah Lutman & Rob Rudolph, Carol & Aaron Mack Charitable Fund of the Minneapolis Foundation, George & Olga Mack, Joshua Mack, Gillian McCain, Mary & Malcolm McDermid, Sjur Midness & Briar Andresen, Peter Nelson & Jennifer Swenson, Marc Porter & James Hennessy, Jeffrey Scherer, Jeffrey Sugerman & Sarah Schultz, Maureen Millea Smith & Daniel Smith, Marla Stack & Dave Powell, Nan G. & Stephen C. Swid, Patricia Tilton, Stu Wilson & Melissa Barker, Warren D. Woessner & Iris C. Freeman, Margaret & Angus Wurtele, and Joanne Von Blon.

For more information about the Publisher's Circle and other ways to support Coffee House Press books, authors, and activities, please visit www.coffeehousepress .org/support or contact us at info@coffeehousepress.org.

Coffee House Press began as a small letterpress operation in 1972 and has grown into an internationally renowned nonprofit publisher of literary fiction, essay, poetry, and other work that doesn't fit neatly into genre categories.

Coffee House is both a publisher and an arts organization. Through our *Books in Action* program and publications, we've become interdisciplinary collaborators and incubators for new work and audience experiences. Our vision for the future is one where a publisher is a catalyst and connector.

Amanda Nadelberg Recommends

The Pink Institution
by Selah Saterstrom

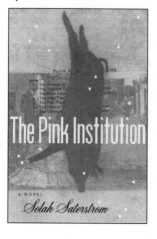

Faces in the Crowd
by Valeria Luiselli

*You and Three Others Are
Approaching a Lake*
by Anna Moschovakis

Leaving the Atocha Station
by Ben Lerner

Songs from a Mountain was designed by
Bookmobile Design & Digital Publisher Services.
The text is set in Minion Pro, an original
typeface designed by Robert Slimbach in 1990.